True love

Psychology of Family Relations-the Psychology of Love

Brenda Lowery

All the people in some moments of life are thinking about relationships with the opposite sex. Why did I choose such a partner? What is the basis of our relationship? What are the roots of a happy family?

Table of Contents

Family Relationship

Modern marriages are increasingly ending in divorce. This is due not only to economic progress, for which the family ceased to be a means of survival:

she can maintain herself and he can arrange a personal life. The birth of children outside of marriage or single-parent family is no longer censured by society, but divorce has never been easier.

The psychology of family relations of husband and wife is an important science that allows us to avoid the crises of family life, in case you began to study it before the start of a relationship. The most important thing in a relationship is to respect the principle of gradualism and build them step by step from the foundation to the roof. Beginning from the moment of love to creation of family.

If we get involved in relationships without knowing how to create them, it is quite likely that at some stage you would find yourself in a crisis in your family life. You will start to feel that something is wrong, and then everything evolves or rather degrades, and the relations of wife and husband is getting worse and worse.

Why do I Dave Such a Partner?

You often hear the familiar lament: why did it have to be him/her? People wonder how they choose the partner who does not meet their expectations.

A woman that left a family of alcoholics didn't want her husband to be drinking, was looking for a partner and still chose the alcoholic. A man that gave himself a vow, the son of a cold and distant mother, that he would marry only a kind and helpful girl and in spite of everything, finds selfish and cold wife.

The child models from the relationship with the parents. Depending on how the child is treated by parents, and what role was assigned to him in the family scenario, the child subconsciously delayed the stereotype of normal relations in the family.

For example, a girl Vanessa grew up in a family where the weak-willed dad always drank, and the mother was always unhappy, often sought the support of the young daughter. The family had argues because of father's alcoholism and the girl had to be "arbitrator" in these quarrels. What kind of relationship will build a mature Vanessa with his partner?

The girl will be attracted to weak men with different kinds of dependencies and always keep "saving" during relationships and at the same time be angry at the partner for its apathy and inertia. It is a pattern of normal relations.

Boy Edgar was a gifted and intelligent child, but his domineering mother did not allow him to take the initiative in many cases, while actively pointing out his mistakes. His father was a silent shadow, in all agreeing with his wife. Little Edgar will grow and will do anything you want, as if breaking out of the cell, but in the end marries a despotic dominant woman who will nag and criticize. Why? Because it will be normal for him.

You need to understand your own childhood. Only by understanding what mistakes were made by your parents, you will be able to understand how it could affect your life. Critically reviewing the relationship with your parents in childhood, you will be able to understand what the relationship is between entrenched you have in the subconscious.

Here are some questions to help:

- Did your parents respected your opinion and listen to you?

- Were you allowed to cry, to feel sad, to grieve, be "bad"?

- Could you easily tell the parents about your problem?

- Did you have a family that was considered normal and genuinely shared their thoughts and experiences?

- Did you get the confidence that parents can decide everything, and you are protected?

If you are answered "no" on two or more questions, most likely you've reached a "toxic" relationship model from childhood, and you need to deal with the psychology of family relationships, the former in the family home and available now in your family.

What can we advise to Vanessa, who is always looking for her weak-willed father in every man? She needs to understand that her attraction to "unhappy" partners stems from children's psychological trauma, where this little girl had to take responsibility for the lives of adults and solve their problems that objectively she was not able to solve. She needs to shift the responsibility for spoiled childhood to her parents, to overcome this loss and continue to live. Remembering that now she doesn't have anyone to protect, it is responsible only for his life, and not in her power to "save" an adult person from any addiction.

Guy Edgar is not necessarily diluted with a domineering wife. He, like Vanessa, needs to understand what his model of toxic relationships are. Realizing that he loses his family in a scenario twitched silent boy Edgar will learn to defend their interests, exercise the will, to express his real feelings, to look for compromises in relations with his wife. If he wishes to keep his family together and can listen and hear his wife, these relations can develop in a harmonious marriage.

Remember, the psychology of family relationships begins with questions to ask yourself. Ask them:

-How do emotions cause me to communicate with my partner?

- What do I bring into this relationship, what role do I play?

- Do I get everything I want from this relationship?

- What prevents me from getting everything I want?

Family Relations: Where is the Source of a Happy Marriage?

All people want a happy family, where partners would act together, and children live airily and happily. It is in our power to build such a family and to secure a safe harbor in the form of an understanding and loving partner. The basis of long-term relationships is love. This is a common truth. But here is a small trick that can sometimes play a key role in the psychology of family relations. Imagine, your beloved person tells you: "I love you for being so clever (smart)." Recognition of your merits can be pleasant but compare: "I love you for what you just are." Love without conditions, accepting a person completely, with all its qualities, even negative, without trying to remake. Unconditional love is the source of harmonious relations in the family.

Naturally, we all certainly love our loved ones. However, most of us rarely expresses this love, and some people even broadcast their partners and children of opposite things:

"You're not behaving, I do not want to love you",

"I want you to lose weight, then I'm back in love with you",

" you hurt me, I do not love you. "

It's like love - it's a bargaining chip in the interpersonal relations market and by making a mistake, you can lose this love.

What should I do? Speak to your loved ones as often as possible about love. Not to discuss their identity. Judge actions, not people. Not to blackmail with love. Here are some examples of phrases that should talk to your partner as often as possible:

-I am very interested in you.

- I love you, even if I'm mad at you.

-I'm upset with your actions, but I will always love you.

- I love you regardless of your actions.

-I will support you in your decision, even if I don't agree with it.

Unconditional love — something that gives us an opportunity to rest, allowing us to be ourselves. This is a condition which many of us did not have in childhood. When we were forced to bear the burden of responsibility for our parents were obliged to conform to ideas about the "right" child, didn't receive respect and acceptance from adults — the list can be long. Each person has his own "history", but the cure is awareness of the experience of his childhood and the unconditional love for your loved ones. This is the basis of the psychology of family relations. These two things can change your home environment in a better way. It means this will be a little change for the better, and the whole world.

What is the Family?

Family — is a group of people, connected with related or marriage bonds, which live under one roof that lead the general economy and having a total budget. Husbands and their children usually serve as the basis of the family. Each of the family members has their responsibilities, which they must carry out for the common advantage.

What kind of family will be determined by a wide range of factors? This affects both the education of spouses and their cultural level. Also, of great importance is the ability of partners to understand each other, to find common solutions in conflict situations, and to show concern and patience.

Some reasons for unhappy marriage.

Many complain that the partner with whom they created a family does not justify their expectations. It turns out that a girl, who suffered during her childhood because her father was an evil, selfish alcoholic, married a similar scoundrel. Why is that happen?

The psychology of family life argues that the foundation of such relationships is laid in childhood. This relationship between parents gives to the child an image of what marriage is about. It turns out that subconsciously, people looking for a partner like one of their parents, continuing an endless cycle of the same mistakes. Because children of these people create a family based on the experience of the parents and continuing the negative traditions of their ancestors.

Another problem is that often people try to create a family, not knowing each other properly. They are driven by passion or an unexpected pregnancy. However, most of these families will fall apart in the first year of marriage. Family psychology teaches that before to take this relationship to such a serious level, you need to know your partner, take it as you are.

Family Love

Initially choosing a partner, people are motivated by his external qualities such as their sexual attractiveness. The sweet voice of the romantics of the divine nature of their feelings in most cases - a pathetic attempt to sugarcoat the harsh reality. Only after the people formed a strong emotional bond and they should learn the inner world of each other, there is love. Everyone says that family is built on love, but why do so many people suffer from lack of warmth and understanding?

The fact is that rarely a person's love just for the fact that he is taking all its advantages and disadvantages.

Usually love is given as a reward for good deeds. The partner sometimes gives threats to deprive their partner if they are not going to match some ideal model. Foundations of family psychology are to love your partner with all their qualities, good and bad. For example, instead of constantly biting his wife for her shortcomings, it is better to focus on the good qualities as often as possible in expressing sympathy and concern.

Another issue of family life is the wrong resolution.

Thus, you will have the skill to work together; you will learn mutual respect and translate their relations to a new level. Often, major conflicts or contradictions within the family are resolved in favor of one spouse or not solved at all. This situation leads to the accumulation of mutual discontent and dissatisfaction with each other. The couple must work together to resolve disputes or conflict situations, listen to the spouse, and respect their opinion.

If family problems are unable to be solved on their own, but there are reasons to save a marriage, then good help may be a trip to a family therapist. Third party people will be able to more objectively assess the real state of things than angry partners.

If you decided to see a specialist, then be honest with them, only then their help will have a chance to succeed. It is better to consult a qualified psychologist. Individuals should beware of questionable doctors practicing unscientific and suspicious methods. If you have a friend of the family, which has received help from such a specialist, listen to their feedback and, if positive, refer to the same specialist.

Crises of Family Life for Years

If we get involved in relationships without knowing how to create them, it is quite likely at some stage, we find ourselves in a situation of crisis of family life. You start to feel that something is wrong, then everything evolves, or rather degraded, and the relations of wife and husband getting worse and worse. What to do at this point?

When you analyze the crises, think about it — relationships do not fall apart overnight, dramatically. It's always a process and a rather long one. It generally it takes as long as the building and development of relationships.

There is no way that husband and wife live in perfect harmony, all of them perfectly, and then BAM— there is a crisis, and the entire relationship collapsed for a couple of weeks. No, of course not. It is always a long period, when people gradually begin to be dissatisfied with each other.

If you suddenly realized that relations have started to develop a bad scenario, and the husband doesn't act the way you dreamed of is the very first awareness of the crisis. This is the first step to correction and improvement.

But realizations that something in your relationship wrong is still not enough. The next step is to determine how this "something" has gone too far. You need to understand what stage of crisis you are in. Below is a list of all the stages of degradation and destruction of the family.

1. The First Crisis — Irritation

This is the starting point of the destruction of the relationship, and it is even hard to call a "crisis." Like nothing happens, but the husband with the wife periodically begin to experience each other irritation.

Where is there irritation? From uncertainty in the husband or wife, worry in the pair. People are sort of already living family, full of harmony, there is a certain inner anxiety. While not much was shown.

What is annoying the husband and wife? The answer is everything. They are just not yet mature enough to relationships in the family, understand family psychology, and not ready.

Because to create relationships, the man needs to understand some basic things about his wife. For example, the fact that she can get very easily upset just for no reason and to looks for the cause makes no sense. This is a woman; she can do it just like that. Thus in 90% of cases, the disorder of women depends on her husband, only about 10% of its impact. The question is whether the husband can tolerate negative emotions from wife all the time. If you are not ready, then it is just too early to get married. You need to be able to tolerate any manifestation of women.

Unfulfilled Expectations

In the case that the relationship begins with the fact that the submissions of the husband or wife don't come true, they begin to think: "this is not the way I imagined our relationship" — that starts the degradation. It's suffering from unrealistic expectations and from the fact that no relationship was built gradually.

Usually, at this stage of the crisis, the man doesn't really want somewhere to aspire to. He doesn't have a global purpose or interests. There is no motion vector. It is simply not necessary. The format of a simple sexes every day, fresh borscht, and work-home-work looks normal. For the women this format is destructive. She doesn't like it, and she doesn't want to live like that.

A woman always wants development. Moreover, this development in the format: someone needs to do something for me, and I'll tell everyone.

The wife begins not to trust her husband, annoyed, and her mistrust reinforces his apathy and passivity. A vicious circle. For example, often the woman asks "what if his targets suck? And I don't like?". Here I want to ask the question, "how can you marry a person, `whom you don't like?". As the time for marriage comes when the purpose of men — this is your goal. That is, you have a common vector, a common desire.

How to Get Out of the First Crisis Relations?

There are several options how to get out of such a fracturing of relations:

1. Try to develop relationships and to build them correctly;

2. To continue to live in same mode, endure, and wait for something unknown;

3. Fan out and look for another husband or wife;

It is important to understand that the second option will only lead to slow death of your relationship, and the next steps in the crisis of your family.

Remember what matters most - your behavior means a lot to men, but if there is harmony at the level of signs, the relationship will be very intense.

The third is possible, but if you will try to find a replacement, not realizing the lessons that gave you life — your new passion will be an exact copy of the previous husband, and probably worse. Only the first option gives a chance for the future harmony in the family.

2. The Second Crisis — Aggressive Husband and the Secretive Wife

If a woman stops trusting her husband, she gradually rose from him, hides his emotions. Closes starts to be silent and starts looking for support elsewhere.

Who can speak for women support? And this is a very serious psychological crisis.

Sometimes she begins to rely on their young children, and it's very sad. Sometimes this support she finds in her father or brother.

When the woman starts to think that her husband is not the best option is really is in fact already cheating. Although there is no physical adultery, mentally a woman in this situation is unfaithful to her husband.

And the man, though rather "unfeeling brute", is the ratio of women — feel and this is becoming more aggressive. Because it invests its time and some strength in a woman who is not his. If he doesn't want to listen — to ask him about it.

His wife starts telling him about the fact that my boss is so cool that a friend's man is better at it, here's another friend — he did great. And man, of these comparisons frantic.

3. The Third Crisis of the Relationship — the Man Becomes Greedy, and the Wife Starts to Cheat

At this stage, the man begins to show the pettiness, greed and excessive greed. This happens for the same reason: the man understands instinctively that the woman was not his — and just doesn't want to invest in it in any way.

That is, if this happens in your relationship, when a woman says: "he was generous, and now has changed" — then you need to look for the node in which occurred the transition of her husband in being who you've become uninteresting. Maybe the wife just never thanked the husband?

The Discord in the Relationship of Husband and Wife

If a husband starts to behave in a similar way, the woman, besides being locked away from men, begins even to deceive him. Some women can be masters in terms of deceptions and tricks and can effectively begin to trace the man around her finger. But the man, though not understood by the mind that something is wrong, begins to feel that it is diluted. Though a man may not able to understand the hints of women, or any subtexts, but when his wife starts to cheat — he wakes up this inner feeling that signals to him about it.

Again, this is turning into another vicious circle, and the psychological crisis is growing — the greedy man, the more the woman is lying, lying more than a woman — the greedier to be the man.

If at this level the relationships are not altered, and the husband and wife begin to rectify the situation, everything becomes worse and goes into the next crisis.

4. The Fourth Crisis — a Husband Becomes ill, and the Wife Becomes Jealous

The husband at this stage begins to go to the limits. He may start to yell at his wife and children and may even begin to dismiss his hands. He may start to seriously hurt the wife, making cruel comments about her appearance and personal qualities. Also, the husband begins to find fault with his wife, constantly making comments to her about her actions and behavior. It turns into a never-ending thread that's just oppressing the woman and it humiliates her.

Husband and Wife Live the Same Life

The wife at this stage, finally loses faith in happiness and starts to become envious gossip, discussing behind her husband all their problems and hardships. Jealous is primarily those who have family life is better, and secretly looked forward to their disorders and the deterioration of relations. All the criticism — first and foremost her husband.

This is a crisis, which is already difficult to change something and somehow under peening relationship. We can say that the relationship is virtually destroyed. Everyone in this relationship, both husband and wife accuses each other, and do not consider that they bear any responsibility for the failure of the marriage.

If you delay such a crisis, and not to leave him drastic measures man is a real loser, sinking lower, and maybe trite to sleep. And the woman stresses more and more and begins to fear everything around her, She starts to panic and her self-esteem sinks to such a low level as to raise it from this level it is unlikely that someone will succeed. Either it will take a very serious effort.

The best solution at this stage is just part, not even necessarily deciding about divorce or separation. It is going to be a long time until the passions subside, and the husband with his wife will be able to speak intelligently without emotions. If later after they had separated, the husband meets the wife and they begin to build relationships from the very beginning — we still have a chance. But it takes time and this time may be long.

The Psychology of Family Relations of Husband and Wife

The degradation of the family is not happening in one moment in your power to turn everything around. Do not make movements, think about the fact that even if in a relationship has crisis and is all bad — that if you just run away in a new relationship, nothing will change. After all, you learned nothing, and did not understand how to behave. Understand that you will need to screw them first and foremost and try to work out on your husband — if you start to act properly, then there is a chance that you will notice changes. So, step by step to rectify the situation.

If this does not help, and your workouts will fail — maybe you should think about the fact that life is not eternal, and you still have a chance to meet your man.

Responsibility and Acceptance of the Role of Men and Women in the Family

Some people believe that they may want to allocate roles between themselves and their family.

It is possible to speak not about the ideal but about the nature of the scheme that underlie the interaction. In this scheme, the natural role, of course, are not the subjects of the agreement. They obviously are not the same for men and women. It follows from biology, and the social nature of the psyche and existence. For example, a man is more suited for operational activities.

Operates better, i.e. men are better at doing what should be done by hand because women and men are different, respectively, and the role they have is different.

Between men and women there are certain differences in mentality. This difference has evolved over hundreds of thousands of years of evolution. Males do the same activities in life, in nature, in the forest — the necessary analytical mentality. Collecting fuel for the fire, it must be good to distinguish dry from wet twigs (or rotten). Preparing a dart or spear for throwing at prey, it must be well to distinguish the difference in weight of the tip and the shaft. Therefore, men are much more developed logical structural thinking is to combine like with like, compare the properties of objects.

The man in the family is the breadwinner and protector. It is its natural function, and not voluntarily adopted by themselves on a conditional role. It sounds corny, but only because these words are so very well-worn. It is not because they are wrong. This is indeed the case — the man is the breadwinner and protector.

In modern life this feature of men seems to be vague and optional. Modern life in civilized countries is far more firmly than in the past, a much higher level of security, there are powerful social institutions. A woman can raise a child herself. So, it seems that you can change roles or change them as you want. Alas, it is illusion. Natural device mentality is a very strong thing and is deep-seated in our psyche. The attempts to ignore this device cannot pass with impunity. Yes, the man today is not necessary to directly produce food and to protect the family from external threats. But the foundation of these men's functions is a liability, and this basis will not go away. It is still relevant today and always will be relevant.

Masculinity is a responsibility. The man responsible for the result. Not to explain why it did not work, even though he was doing everything right. No, the man responsible for the fact that, in the end, it turned out. And if it did not, so he was doing something wrong. A responsible man will not say, "You're wrong to have brought up children". Where have you been? Worked? So, you went to the child brought your wife, so as he can, as it sees fit. Now answer for it me do not blame her.

What is the typical female role? The female lead, the female mentality is, again, not some arbitrary, but biologically and mentally conditioned phenomenon.

In our psyche there are two different "floors". The main floor is a natural psyche. It differs from the animal, it develops first in our infancy and life remains the basis of our existence, responsible for a huge number of actions and manifestations. The second floor is higher psyche, purely human. The one where you have no animals. These floors are different from each other a lot of different things but are the main difference, the most fundamental.

It consists in the fact that the person is aware in the fact of its own existence, and the animal does not give. The chicken does not understand that she is one of the chickens, and the monkey doesn't understand that she's one of the monkeys. And each of us understands that it is the same as the rest of the people. The other side of this same human ability to imagine other people's feelings. "I can be good or bad, so now someone also wants to eat". "Once I can be warm or cold, so now someone maybe freezes".

The ability to imagine other people's feelings is called empathy (for animals, this is not possible; they cannot imagine the feelings of other individuals). And on this basic distinction of the human psyche from the animal, women are man than a man. She has the most empathy developed fundamentally better. Why? For the same purely biological reasons.

Unlike women, men have the power and the possibility of solving problems in the relationship. Away, to hit, to kill, to escape. Women have no such possibility. So, the man is not very important to grasp the intricacies of the status of the partner and the woman is vital. It is much more focused on the perception of the nuances of facial expressions, intonation, rhythm, breath, that which gives the human condition. Therefore, women are much more empathic; it is easier to understand the partner.

And the more you understand the person, the more you take, the more feel his experiences; better understand what pushes him to actions, including "bad".

Therefore, the adoption is women's role in the family. Unconditional acceptance, motherhood, femininity.

Now we can generalize these two roles in any pair "man and woman". Male, female — unconditional acceptance. That's when both partners are best suited to these roles, it is often very good, and around them is very good. This is one of the criteria that shows whether people are allied with each other. When the pair emerged on the right, "benign", the people around to feel good about. They have improved relationships with others, are drawn to them.

And sometimes otherwise, when the two teamed up to any protest basis. Both bad, both lonely. For example, some of them do not have a relationship with heavy parents. And it is from under these parents ran away to the partner, whom it adopted, comforts, unites with him in the General protest. Here such people as were still bad relations with others and continue to deteriorate.

Induction and Deduction

Let's start with how women think. The main feature of female logic is **the inductance**. That is, in his discussion girls usually erect any private situation to the rank of a kind of "eternal laws." The classic example of this are phrases like: "He was not paying me time," or "We never are". In cases where the reason for such generalizations is only one or a few such incidents.

Because of the tendency for women to generalize and simplify certain situations many men hard to understand them. In result come out only quarrels and insults. As is often in the eyes of men favorite accusations seem completely unfounded. Men is difficult to accept the fact that for one offense the second half ready to wipe out all the old tokens.

In addition, the male brain used to do it completely differently. Men's thinking is closest to **the deductive** method. This means that they, on the contrary, moving from the General to the. For example, most men would be perfectly natural thought: "If all women who love perfume and my will definitely enjoy this gift." And then it comes the turn of the offended woman. Because almost every woman on Earth, no matter what nationality it was, and no matter what worldview are not adhered to, will not allow it compared with others.

We Speak Different Languages

Sometimes even in a simple conversation men and women find it difficult to understand each other. They use the same language and understandable words. So, what's the problem? The essence of the misunderstanding that men in everyday conversations are focused on understanding the words in their direct meaning. If they say, "a lot", it means "a lot". While women may exaggerate, use metaphors and similes.

The woman in the conversation is important to convey your feelings and emotions. Because women are more open and much more likely than men to talk about their feelings. And most importantly – they can perceive information, based on feeling, not rational judgment. So, for them the clarity of replicas usually remains in second place. Women rarely focus on how to convey the facts with absolute precision. They need to speak out, to throw out the emotions that overwhelm.

For men the main thing is to get information. They are interested in the essence. So, whatever was discussed, the representative of the stronger sex is most important to formulate precisely the thought, to choose the right and meaningful words. For this reason, they are rarely able to properly understand women's statements: "NOBODY loves Me!" or "I'm tired of ALL my work!" Men will take the words "no one" and "all" in the literal meaning, whereas the woman did not mean it.

The Reason for Our Differences?

Recently, scientists have discovered an interesting fact. It turns out that men have more developed right hemisphere of the brain and in females the left. Although previously it was believed the contrary. That is why women are so different.

The right hemisphere is responsible for abstract thinking, spatial orientation and emotions. While the left is for communication, analytical thinking and memory. Why women are more talkative and aim to create a different kind of relationship. Whereas men due to their emotional more focused on action and competition. Of these features and follow all the basic differences between women and men.

Despite gender differences, men and women can't live apart. Because they complement each other. However, sometimes differences become a barrier to the creation of strong and harmonious relationships. What to do in this case?

The main weapon against misunderstandings will be the knowledge. After all, most quarrels occur since one or both partners don't know anything about male and female differences. So, they hope such behavior, which could expect from themselves.

Studying the psychology of the opposite sex, everyone can become a little bit more bearable for the other half. The key is to learn to understand that you need a person in every situation. And to put yourself in the place of a loved one or beloved.

Who is the Boss in the Family?

The main issue is the stumbling block for most families — who is the boss in the family? Traditionally, the male in some sense is in charge and the woman is struggling to not to agree with it itself to be superior or at least equal.

The flaw in all these arguments is the word "home". What do you mean "main"? The one who says: "in my opinion- and everything!" insists on its decision, just to make a point? In this sense, no one should be in charge. This position is motivated by a real authority, not more life experience, and self-doubt, fear to expose the real discussion of his views and intentions.

But if the word "home" be something reasonable, then it's the same responsibility. The main — one who is in the end responsible for the decisions taken.

Example: Husband and wife came to the airport 45 minutes before departure. The wife says: "I'd like little shops in duty-free". If the husband agrees, and then they miss the plane, it should not afford the slightest irritation, don't have to swear and complain about the wife. He should say: "I'm burdock, it will be necessary next time to keep track of time". And next time (or not putting this "experiment"), to say to his wife: "No, sorry, I can't allow that to happen. There is no opportunity to go shopping, you risk being late". He takes on the role of "chief" not in the sense of pressure and sense of responsibility.

If a man should be responsible, how to behave as a woman to help him do it: what prevents a man to take responsibility for themselves?

Self-doubt, fear. But here, it is necessary to clarify the fear of what.

At first glance, fear of mistakes, of loss. "I go to school and talk to the teacher of the child, and I can't do that". The fear of possible failure. Actually no. Not such fear. Because this fear is everywhere including quite responsible people. Any of us understand what could be wrong or not to achieve success. So, a turn out irresponsibility is not the fear of his failure, and fear of others ' reaction to this failure.

To understand what others, let's remember whose reaction was the first in our lives? Of course, parents.

I remember one of my companions — almost tycoon, who was dismantled cog of the TV at age 9 and not be able to collect back. His parents a word of reproof did not say, although the TV was a very important thing. And in 14 years he has worked in telepathic as master. And 40 was already a very successful businessman.

Now, a woman can help a man become more responsible, if it is in accordance with its main female lead will be a source of unconditional acceptance. If it is in any situation is to treat the husband is not estimated, and sympathetic, particularly in his failure. Somewhere he missed, someone he had failed, for something not his own took — she should not respond to his actions ("well, how are you?"), and to his feelings ("how did you become nervous!") Then he gradually, over the years, gets rid of the fear that prevents him from taking responsibility.

Here is an example from life, as the wife "molded" her husband. Got him for his birthday the digital camera when they first came out. Such thin and tiny. The whole family chipped in for a gift, money then was not special. And he did not part with it, shooting recklessly, wore it on the lace on the chest. Once at a party, at the table, he began to show the camera his neighbor. And with drunken eyes, dropped it in a bowl with Lecho. And, behold, he is beside himself with grief, pulls out a bowl of Lecho this camera, it drains the marinade, and the wife immediately, without hesitation, said: "Jasper, you are so photographic, almost in the extreme conditions that it should be considered a baptism of fire." See, for her this attitude on autopilot, she doesn't have to think. This is what is called unconditional acceptance.

In such an atmosphere the man becomes afraid. Ceases to not be afraid of their failures, and reactions to these failures. Begins to take responsibility.

We considered the situation, when they agreed; the man took on this responsibility and is responsible for the consequences. But the process of discussion. As we found out, the male logic, female intuition. They are different and often want different things.

Here the most important thing is to set a goal. Usually in such cases it seems that the goal is to convince, to persuade, to push. To succeed. In fact, to negotiate with someone, especially with an opponent, it is necessary first to ensure a truly friendly tone of the conversation. This is the most difficult, but it is most important. Due to the lack of this objective, due to the tense tone of us and do not hear, do not go towards us trying, on the contrary, we push.

And for proper intonation you need to understand that the other person does not mean purposely to contradict. How it would otherwise may seem, no matter how it seemed that he (she) said purposely, on purpose, just to hurt me. It is not so! For his (her) perseverance is a sort of inner conviction, genuine concern, and irritability or even rude — a request.

And it is necessary to reckon with the conviction. We need to prove that you see that concern and considered her. "Tell me, Leo, why are you not allowed to buy his son a cell phone? You think it's too expensive? You think it'll spoil? ». If the wife asks it without calling, without reproach, but with a genuine interest in his reasons, the intensity of emotions is greatly reduced.

For husband and wife, it's all quite symmetrical. "Tell me, Melissa, you really think it's important to buy him the cell phone? You're afraid that otherwise it will feel like the black sheep among your classmates?" To ask without calling, without antics. Then further conversation will allow her husband to present their counter-considerations, and hope that it will be heard.

Well, emotions removed. But still, one wants one, another wants another. This means that one must give away, to make a sacrifice.

Here it is necessary to speak not about the negotiation process and about the substance of the relationship between these two men. It is necessary to understand, who to whom it refers. In the relations of men and women have two different starters, two completely different feelings. One of these feelings — the need to it was good as it is in my hands. And quite another, opposite feeling — this need to be fine as far as it depends on it.

In real life there are, of course, both beginning in every person, and in any pair. It's quite normal feeling, the need to be happy. A question only in proportions, the only question is what kind of feeling is now stronger than my motivation, what a feeling louder pronounced. This proportion depends on the maturity of man: the more mature the person, the more he can focus on your partner.

Unfortunately, or fortunately, the psyche is so constituted that partner significantly only have feelings that prevails. If I pull the blanket over myself, the partner discreetly (or whatever) that in some cases I'm still considered with him. And here is the real background, who to whom it refers, it comes out only in situations of conflict, only in a situation of conflict of interests.

While both indulge in things that do not infringe upon anybody's interests such as going shopping, going to the rally, blamed the bad weather or skiing — in these serene situations nothing can be said about the true nature of their relationship. But when one wants to sleep and another to listen to loud music — here is someone whose interests ahead of values.

In an ideal family, each striving to the other, each trying to pull the blanket off himself and put it on the other. Everyone thinks — not cold there different.

A man should be responsible. When he manifests, he becomes head of the family.

The woman becomes the head of the family when she takes a very immature man. It assumes — correctly recognizes its immaturity. And it is this immaturity touched, not annoyed, not disappointed. She feels its potential she felt sorry for him. And she wants to help him to deploy his potential. She takes it and starts to gently, patiently guide him through life. In this case, the woman becomes "benign", the proper head of the family. She takes responsibility for what is happening.

A «Poor» family is just when there is a struggle for the leadership and these scenes most in our families. Why is this happening?

Men traditionally feel comfortable being head of the family. He feels in his place, when he is the leader. Why woman fighting for leadership in the family? Just by the fact that there are many different reasons.

For example, when a woman is terribly uncomfortable with this man, and she's just trying to get out from under the wreckage and somehow prove their own right to an opinion on where I should go or not go. It is not a struggle for leadership, the struggle for life.

Sometimes the struggle for leadership is when the woman in psycho, by psycho-physical data is a potentially powerful manager. Among women, it is not common, but occurs. And then this managerial capacity distorted, ugly begins to be realized in a family struggle for priority.

"Powerful Manager" From Nature

The right manager (i.e., from nature, not from neurosis) is the person who the psycho is prone to structuring a situation for its improvement, optimization. He has such a need, and there's nothing he can do about it. He first says, "Let's table otherwise put here then more people will sit down", "let's open the window, and stuffy".

Wrong, the neurotic Manager is not concerned about the improvement of the situation and his superiority. He may also say about the window, but only to be the first to say that to score points.

There is a mixture of the other. The most vital character is mixed. This is when a person, on the one hand, a Manager by nature, their mindset: Manager, organizer, leader. And on the other side he, due to his childhood situation, it remains under-loved, so not a confident person. And being on your leadership place makes large elements of the dictates of the individual, intolerance. So, here's a woman fighting for power in the family, can be such a character. It can be from the nature of the right Manager, organizer, Manager, but not psychologically intact person. And therefore, its inclination so ugly manifested in the family.

How a man can help a woman to occupy its rightful place? We have seen how a woman can help a man just to play a role of course the host female. The man is just as likely to help a woman playing a role — i.e. to be the most responsible, "to take". And then the woman has a sense of security, which will help her, in turn, be unconditionally accepting. Often, it leaves him the field for acceptance of responsibility. She decides everything, and he doesn't even have time to take responsibility. Decides everything, did it.

Usually, it happens when a man, apparently pissed off about this, internally still willing to put up with it: "Well, in the end, what's so terrible". If he realizes that it's bad for everyone, bad for her, in the end, he fearlessly stops, turns even far-reaching process, cancelling the invited guests, going on a monetary loss, for return of tickets instead of saying to the wife: "come on will, in my opinion".

The best thing to say to the wife: "Let's not make the decision alone. Let's not think and it is not, in my opinion, let's discuss and negotiate. And that we continue to move definitely will not".

The concept of male (female) work in the family

For this, it is not necessary to go to a professional psychologist. This follows from common sense.

I know examples when a woman begins to earn, and the man stays at home and does housework. And even claims that he likes it. Can it be considered normal in such a situation? No, you cannot.

The man, to feel good, as, indeed, and a woman, engages in some activity, look for ways of self-realization. Nothing living does not tolerate static: that does not develop, it will inevitably deteriorate.

If a man is sitting at home for a long time and not growing, it is only a short time can go on. Outwardly all looks well — groomed children the apartment in order. But with the months it starts to deteriorate character. He is becoming more irritable, or more autistic, less topics of conversation interests him, eyes glaze over... a Situation where the man stays at home and does nothing, normally it can only be a short transitional stage, the search for new forms of relationship, work, himself, when he continues to act, and under the new, does not know how.

When a woman stays home with children, it is the same thing happens. Moreover, it appears that mothers have worse relationships with their children, when they sit at home and not working. It would seem, an unexpected conclusion, but the survey lead to it...

A woman may not be in order if it doesn't work, but this does not mean that she must make a career. We must look for activities that she is most peculiar. Activities in which it will deal with the most pleasure that will feel more natural. This is called self-realization. If the woman has no understanding of what kind of activities, then the first thing necessary to start — to learn something. Whatever it is, again, just to maintain an intellectual tone. Though owning a computer, though the history of painting. For a start, 2-3 times a week for an hour, on the Internet, with teacher, with friends. And the toning learning — mathematics and languages. All this is quite possible to do sitting at home and raising children.

When people marry, very often fall into the illusion that enter a relationship with this person — a woman or a man, and only him. It is a deep and dangerous delusion. You enter a relationship not with this or Jodie Anthony, and with the enormous complex, the core of which(s) he is. It is the parents of this man, and his relationship with his parents, and his relationship with work, money, his previous women, wives-husbands, with his children in the previous marriage. It is all important to get before marriage to weigh whether you want that person in real the totality of the circumstances. For the marriage was successful, you will have to interact with this complex. And if the woman was inside this family situation, the family the role of wife, not just to build relationship with your husband and help him to develop this large crystal lattice. That is the most correctly to build relations with his relatives. This is the most important role of his wife. For the husband is symmetrical.

"The famous writer Thomas Clayton Wolf said in one of his works: "You can't go home." We don't come back - instead, we transfer the child to him. We each have a fundamental need to recreate in your life the circumstances of his parents ' family, even if these circumstances were destructive and hurt".

We recommend you read a book from our series about **True love: "Love Before Marriage and in Marriage."**